The Rugs of Teec Nos Pos:
Jewels of The Navajo Loom

adobe gallery
413 romero street nw
albuquerque, nm 87104

To Bernard, and
To the weavers who made this catalog
and exhibit possible

The Rugs of Teec Nos Pos:
Jewels of The Navajo Loom

Ruth K. Belikove

adobe gallery
art of the southwest indian

adobe gallery
art of the southwest indian
ALEXANDER E. ANTHONY JR.
413 romero street nw albuquerque, nm 87104
(505) 243-8485 • (800) 821-5221

Library of Congress Cataloging-in-Publication Data

Belikove, Ruth K.
    The rugs of Teec Nos Pos : jewels of the Navajo loom / Ruth K.
Belikove.
        p.   cm.
    Includes bibliographical references.
    ISBN 0-9633710-1-0
    1. Navajo textile fabrics--Exhibitions. 2. Teec Nos Pos (Ariz.)
3. Belikove, Ruth K.--Ethnological collections--Exhibitions.
    I. Title.
    E99.N3B435 1994
    746.7'2--dc20   94-7094
                                                     CIP

ISBN-0-9633710-1-0

Cover: Teec Nos Pos Rug, 62" x 107," circa 1925 - 1935.
Rugs of the "Golden Age" of Teec Nos Pos weaving are
characterized by massive and standardized borders,
with most variations a back-to-back design or "U"
shape in beige, outlined in black with accents of red and green.
This rug incorporates a second inner border which
dramatically offsets the center field.

Contents

University Art Museum
Nelson Fine Arts Center
Arizona State University

For over forty years the Arizona State University Art Museum has been a vital visual art resource center for Arizona. The museum collects, presents and interprets art from different periods and cultures, with attention to the arts of the Southwest. The showing of the Ruth Belikove collection of Teec Nos Pos Navajo rugs continues this tradition. These outstanding rugs are shown in conjunction with the museum's collection of Navajo rugs from the Castle Hot Springs Resort, which was a prominent winter spot in the 19th and early 20th centuries. These resort rugs were collected haphazardly, as functional objects to be used on the floors, walls and furniture and to enhance the southwestern dude ranch atmosphere.

The Castle Hot Springs collection contrasts markedly with the Belikove collection of Teec Nos Pos rugs, which were collected recently with great care and attention to the history of Navajo rug-making and the distinct Teec Nos Pos style. This exhibition examines the process and intention of collecting, and suggests the impact of this collection on Navajo artists.

The ASU Art Museum is fortunate to present the Belikove collection and to be associated with Ruth Belikove, a dedicated collector and supporter of Native American art and artists.

Heather Sealy Lineberry
Curator
Arizona State University Art Museum

Acknowledgments

Without the vision and appreciation of Marilyn Zeitlin and Heather Lineberry of the Arizona State University Museum, there would be no exhibit and no catalog. This museum will present what may be the first exhibit of regional rugs from the Teec Nos Pos Trading Post on the Navajo Reservation, in the Four Corners area where the states of Arizona, New Mexico, Utah and Colorado meet. The rugs included in this exhibit were made in the first half of the 20th century.

Wonderful worlds opened for me serendipitously after meeting Tyrone Campbell. Our business partnership introduced me to the world of Indian art, to learn, to love, to see — to walk in beauty.

My heartfelt thanks to Andrew Nagen for his encouragement and caring. And to the dealers who brought exceptional rugs to me.

Kathy Foutz has been particularly helpful in developing this research project. We interviewed Russell and Helen Foutz, Bill Foutz of the Foutz Trading Company, Ruthie McGee, and Charles and Grace Herring, who added the Sunday saddle blanket to my collection. Leland Noel shared his encyclopedic family history. These were the highlights of the research and I thank them for sharing their memories.

After many years as a librarian, I know that librarians are always great friends.

Laura Holt at the Laboratory of Anthropology, and the librarians at the School of American Research in Santa Fe, Farmington N.M. Public Library, University of California at Berkeley Libraries, the Heard Museum, Arizona State University, and New Mexico State Archives made contributions to the construction of this publication.

Special recognition to Henrietta Stockel for her advice, support and offer to edit. That we come from the same hometown, Perth Amboy, New Jersey, is insignificant to the fact that we both are totally involved with Native American people — she with the Chiricahua Apaches and I with the art of the Navajo.

Robert Sherwood struggled to carry these heavy rugs to his studio to photograph them to their best advantage. I'm grateful.

My grandchildren, Sasha and Adam Talcott, showed remarkable patience when I needed help with my first venture into word processing. Ken Feehan devotedly put the polish on the manuscript for hours on his computer. A salute to Jeff Robinson who understood my passion for ballroom dancing which served to keep me healthy. Thank you, Carol Ann Mackay!

There are so many friends who touch one's life and who make a difference, that it's almost impossible to mention all of them. My heartfelt thanks are offered to all of those people whose names will not be included here.

Teec rhymes with peace!

Tell Me—Why TEECS?

I'm from New Jersey and I'm running a "fever"! A fever to collect, that is. Never had I come close to a Navajo or to her rug until seven years ago. I didn't know about Indians, even from my school days, and my family home had Oriental, not Navajo rugs on the floor. I had flown over the southwest, but had driven through only once (the obligatory cross-country trip so the children could see...).

After my husband's death in 1977, my life took many twisting and winding turns, eventually to a place which led me into a business partnership buying and selling old Navajo textiles, located in Metuchen, New Jersey. The nature of the business brought me to New Mexico and Arizona and I promptly fell in love. I didn't think I would ever be able to utter more than "ooh, look at that," which could have meant that I was swooning over the color of the sky, the shapes of the clouds or the shifting of the light on the mountains. My soul claimed this beauty for me, making it a kind of nirvana.

"Ooh, look at that" also applies to my approach to Navajo textiles. I looked at blankets and rugs and used those very words (and still do) about these artistic, optical, beautifully designed works of art. So, Ruth—why collect Teecs? What next? Rugs from the 20th century? Rugs from an unpronounceable trading post area in isolated northern Arizona? Since my soul had been responding to these Teec Nos Pos rugs from the beginning of my education, I began to think that I couldn't live without them (the pitfall of every collector—I must have them!). And then I began buying them and haven't stopped.

Do I love these rugs with the designs reminiscent of Oriental rug motifs because I remembered the Oriental rugs from my childhood? Does it matter? For me they represent art in the highest form—perfectly balanced designs, mirror imaged, highlighted with just the right amount of color in just the right places. They nourish my soul. I see wide borders, sometimes in multiples, and an elaborate menu of frets, hooks, stars, bows, arrows, diamonds, triangles and other small designs floating on the well carded field.

My fever has not abated, I'm a happy collector, I love my Teec collection and treasure my luck.

Ruth Belikove

Introduction

Teec Nos Pos, *circle of cottonwoods* (trees). Anyone who has visited the Southwest or spent time on the Navajo Reservation knows the value and opportunity found at a circle of cottonwoods. Cottonwoods mean water, shade, food, fuel, the opportunity to sit and rest, encounter a fellow traveller, or to just think, luxuriating in the assured shade.

At first, Teec Nos Pos came to me at my store in 1976, in the form of Bill Foutz. He chewed gum real hard and told me "I had, just had to buy his rugs. They're the best, Androoo." Wide Ruins* layouts with Teec Nos Pos style panels, Two Grey Hills* colored Teec Nos Pos with Red Mesa* outline and geometric field elements. They were mostly woven of commercial (not handspun wool) yarn. Bill said the Navajo shipped their wool to Boston for cleaning and what came back may not even be the same Navajo wool that the Navajo sent. Such is the color of the reservation.

It is no surprise that the rugs seen in this catalog grew and matured in this particular area of the Navajo Reservation. This oasis, with its opportunity for contemplation, fostered the most complex and communicative of all Navajo 20th century weavings.

Exchange of information is often encouraged among great artists. Upon closer examination, one can see the Plains Indian beadwork designs as borders on Teec Nos Pos rugs. The complex geometric field, attributed to the Oriental carpets or photos made available to weavers, is part of an impersonal exchange. The point may be, when you mix a Caucasian rug with a Navajo mind you get a Teec Nos Pos! How could this come about? Clearly business consideration and sales must have influenced the traders.

* Trading posts on the Navajo Reservation featuring distinctive regional rug designs.

The Teec Nos Pos rug offered a quality, appealing product that could rival or surpass the technical and visual superiority of the Oriental rug.

The comparison of the Teec Nos Pos rugs to Oriental carpets is irresistible. But is it the point? Do we see parallel development here? With rare exception, the Navajo Teec Nos Pos rugs communicate something quite different from their antecedents, though obvious homage is paid to their design systems. They radiate intelligence, balance, clarity, and a remarkable sense of order, without the jumble of their Middle Eastern cousins.

Not all weavers have genius and courage, so the average Teec Nos Pos rugs utilize repetitive geometric border elements in the field as well as the perimeter. However, the best examples contrast border with field like a movie marquee.

What type of woman could begin this new vision? Did her personality or life style allow her creative courage to flow? Parallel development, again, shall we say? The Teec Nos Pos rug most illustrates the continuous thread of the world weaving tradition. How easily the Navajo adapted the Eastern designs to their saddle blankets and rugs.

The Teec Nos Pos weavers were so masterful they exceeded many of the achievements of the earliest weavers. The best Teec Nos Pos rugs rival the best Classic blankets (1830-1860), the best products of their respective days. Characteristically, Teec Nos Pos rugs are: 1.) usually large and narrow, 2.) have unique complex design systems with all elements outlined, 3.) the best often lack a selvage (warp) cord and have reinforced warps at number one warp.

Teec Nos Pos Saddle Blankets are popular among collectors and Native Americans and

were at the zenith of their production in the 1910-1935 period. Sometimes composed with a blank center panel, the "fancy" Teec Nos Pos borders of these blankets were natural embellishments on, under, or in place of the saddle. Why not offer your best designs for your often times, closest, most important four-legged companion? Remember, the Teec Nos Pos borders seem closely linked to the Plains Indian design system (which predates Teec Nos Pos, and was an equestrian culture also). After a Teec saddle, one could not ever return to the ubiquitous, conventional, striped saddle blanket.

Pictorial Teec Nos Pos are rare. Why? Maybe it is because Teec weavers were more oriented to contemporary art and had a unique vision for geometric relationships, rather than folk art. They were beyond the representational. Many of the best examples seem to have advanced knowledge and peer into the future design systems of electronic circuit boards or complex architectural plans. The question I ask of inquisitive sellers about their rug is, "Does it look like a wiring diagram?"

We had a Teec Nos Pos rug, Tyrone and I, called the Dash Board of the Star Ship Enterprise. Hung horizontally, one was beckoned to turn a lever, twist a dial, or await paper output. It was large, approximately 7 x 14 feet, and came out of Canada. I always wondered about the woman who conceived this rug. The timelessness of this piece of art makes it great. Great art from any period will always transcend time. Good yesterday. Good today. Good tomorrow.

Distinct regional Teec Nos Pos weaving seems to appear approximately from 1910-1915 while Red Mesa development occurred in the 1880s. The Oriental rug influence is obvious in the geometric style, but to my thinking and observation, I choose to see another path. The link

in the Red Mesa / Teec Nos Pos style of weaving at its earliest form is the "eyedazzler," circa 1890s, with a single linear border. After experiencing many Transitional Eyedazzlers, we see the coming of the Red Mesa outline rug. When considering the consummate geometric Teec, can we consider the Transitional Period Germantown dazzlers and the earliest rugs from the Red Mesa area? These Germantowns display precision and balance, with multi-color outlining, seen as the 20th century Teec and Red Mesa hallmarks. It would seem that the superior Germantown, non-regional weavers could have parented the regional Teec / Red Mesa weavers and passed along their ideas and talents.

The Navajo were open to letting other cultures influence their design systems. In the early period we see the Mexican influence on the Navajo blanket weavers. When it was time to make the shift to weaving rugs, the Oriental rug design system was a natural place to find inspiration. How interesting the ease with which the Navajo nomads incorporated the designs fostered by their Middle Eastern peers. Upon viewing Bedouin costumes, I am taken by the similarity in design to those of the Teec Nos Pos and Red Mesa areas. Could these nomadic people see the same geometry in their separate, but geographically similar homelands?

I like to talk at lectures about "the continuous thread." It is my hope that after visiting this exhibit, the viewer will come away with a glimpse at one aspect of the continuous thread of the world textile tradition. We have Ruth Belikove to thank for this opportunity.

Andrew Nagen

The Trading Post

Hambleton Bridger Noel exclaimed that Black Horse "was the finest looking man I ever saw, but he had the disposition of a devil!"[1] This influential Navajo, who was neither a chief nor head of a clan, who disliked the white man, controlled the territory where Noel planned to establish his trading post. Ten years before, Black Horse had driven away two prospective traders. It was in 1905, several years after his arrival from Virginia, a victim of tuberculosis, that Hamp Noel, his wagon loaded with trade goods, travelled alone and unarmed across the Arizona desert, probably from Fort Defiance, beyond the Carrizo Mountains to a canyon boasting an abundance of cottonwood trees on T'iisnasbas Creek. Here he founded Teec Nos Pos, Navajo for *cottonwoods in a circle** (or was it here that the wagon broke down?).

The Navajo had word of his coming and upon Noel's arrival, he estimated 1,000 - 1,500 (McNitt thinks it was probably more like several hundred) Navajo gathered in the canyon to decide if they wanted this slight, boyish looking white man to live among them. The discussion took most of the day. Noel said "I gave them food for a big meal, flour, a few muttons and coffee. The squaws cooked it."[2] And they feasted. By evening, the Indians agreed to allow him to build the post.

Meanwhile, Black Horse arrived to see what was going on. When he saw Noel, he recognized him as the *biliganna* (white man) who had befriended him when he was sick and hungry a few years before at Chaco Canyon. Black Horse, an impressive six footer, had a dynamic, charismatic personality and dominated any space he occupied. He was an impassioned speaker. Noel said "when he talked at meetings his words carried weight."[3] Black Horse spoke in favor of Noel.

One of Noel's other strong supporters was Tribal Judge Clah-Chis-Chilli (Left Handed Curly Man) who thought that Hamp Noel would be fair with the Indians. They knew and respected Frank Noel, Hamp's older brother, for his honest dealings as trader at neighboring Sa Nos Tee Trading Post. Clah also pointed out the convenience of having the trading post to avoid travel in bad weather, to buy trade goods, or sell sheep, wool, or hides.

Both Hamp Noel and his father had been born on a plantation near Tappahannock, Virginia, which had been in the family for 70 years. The elder Noel, a surgeon, had served with the Confederate army during the Civil War, practiced medicine privately, and died from tuberculosis at age 50. Hamp's mother, Clara, who came from a prominent Baltimore family, ran the plantation until her own death from tuberculosis in 1891. The family was uprooted and Hamp's three older brothers went west to the Four Corners area where Hamp eventually joined them from Baltimore in 1898. "In Baltimore," he said, "I lived right above a busy street with street cars and all kinds of traffic going by far into the night. I was used to the noise and could sleep like a baby. Out here the silence was too much for me."[4] Noel was already weakened by tuberculosis. The dry New Mexico air was good for him and he began to feel better.

Noel's choices in the territory were either farming or trading with the Indians. He chose the latter. At Teec Nos Pos, he was the only white man within 30 miles. He lived in a hogan while the trading post was being built.

* This is sometimes interchangable with "circle of cottonwoods."

At first, he found it difficult to trust the Navajo. "When I went out to Teec Nos Pos, it was wild country. I knew I was up against it, but didn't want trouble," he once said. "A drummer (peddler) sold me an automatic-loading, high-powered rifle. I took the Navajos out, and we shot a rabbit or at pieces of rock high up in the canyon wall. After a lot of this shooting, and letting the Indians see how I could shoot, I hung the rifle up in the post, on the wall in back of the counter in easy reach and where they could see it. But I never had to take it down in a hurry. There was never any trouble."[5] His prowess as a sharpshooter was honed from hunting as a boy on the plantation.

Noel's contacts with the outside world were severely limited by the lack of roads into the trading post. This isolation lasted until 1959 when the first road was built through Teec Nos Pos. John Wetherill, first from Oljetoh and later from Kayenta (1910), sent his freight wagon across the northern part of the reservation into Teec Nos Pos. The old maps show the route as the Wetherill Trail. Noel stated "that he (Wetherill) sent his loaded wagon to my store, with a return order. Then I would fill his wagons from my post and take his goods on to the C. H. Algert Company, wholesale store in Fruitland, N.M., using my teams."[6] Betty McGee, Noel's daughter, reported that her father also went out in his wagon to sell goods and at these times slept with a gun under his pillow."[7]

In 1907, the superintendent from the regional Indian Bureau, William Shelton, told the Indians that it was mandatory to send their children to school at Shiprock, New Mexico, but they wouldn't comply. Noel reported, "Judge Clah-Chis-Chilli, and three or four Indians came to see me at Teec Nos Pos to tell me there might be trouble, and then went on to see Byalille, head man of the

Old Navajo war chiefs, "BI-LEEN-KLA-ZHIN" (Black Horse) on the left, and "TAI-O-NIE" on the right. Both now deceased. Photo from The Navajo by J.B. Moore, courtesy Sim Schwemberger.

Navajos in this region, living near Aneth, Utah. I was told that if Shelton sent troops to enforce the school order, Byalille's outfit would rob my store, and with the supplies go to Moonlight where there was no road within 100 miles, and hide out. It was implied that they would shoot me and burn my store after robbing it."[8] Shelton had sent for the troops. Just before daybreak, the troops surrounded the camp and took 15-20 prisoners. Noel said "I was not there, but the Indians who were told me about it later. One of the Navajos came out of his hogan with a rifle, went up behind a fence, and shot at one of the troopers and missed. The troops then opened fire and killed this man and one other Navajo. I don't think the soldiers had any casualties. All of the Navajos were arrested and put in a prison a while and then turned loose."[9]

Noel gained the eventual trust and friendship of the Navajos in the area. Betty McGee

In front of every trading post at that time (circa 1949), there was a guest hogan where Indians would stay if they were coming to the store or on their way to some other place. At Teec Nos Pos, a man died in the hogan and they destroyed the hogan immediately. Conversation with Helen Foutz, Farmington, New Mexico, July 1993.
Photo by Milton "Jack" Snow, Courtesy Museum of New Mexico Negative #46042. (Navajo culture exposes a fear of the dead and all their possessions. It is customary to destroy the hogan or hut where anyone has died.)

reports that he respected and encouraged them, and taught them discipline and courtesy (based on his Mormon beliefs). As their teacher he was able to shape their lives and views of the outside world.[10] In those days, the trader wore many hats—lawyer, doctor, marital counselor, teacher, friend, undertaker, and banker (most business was done on credit).

The trading post was the local newsroom for the Indians.

In 1911, at age 35, Hamp Noel married Eva Foutz. By 1913, the tuberculosis recurred as a result of stress and indoor living, and Hamp was confined to bed. From a cot in his living room, he was able

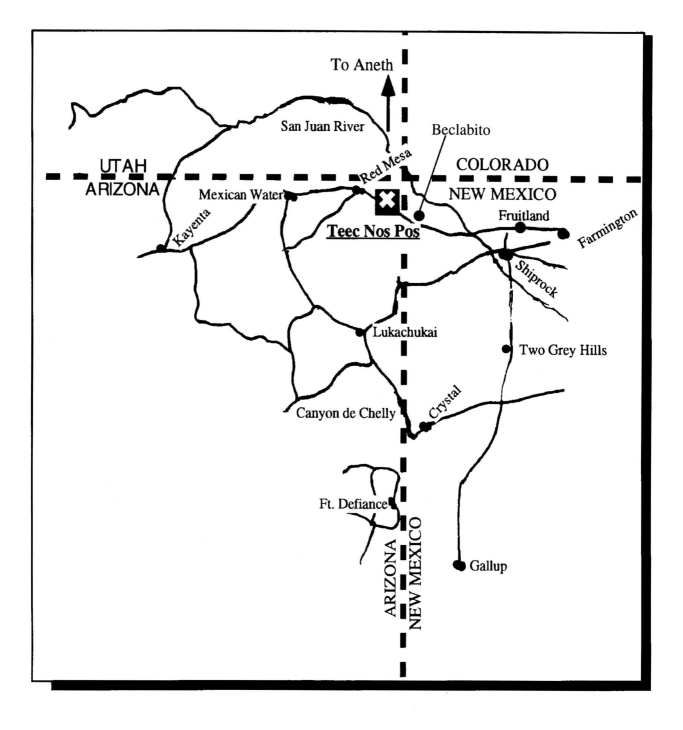

to keep an eye on the activities of the trading post through a peep hole in the wall. Hamp and Eva sold the trading post in 1913 to Bert Dustin and moved their family to a ranch in Fruitland where Hamp lived to his 88th year. (The peep hole was still in place when Russell Foutz and Ken Washburn bought the trading post in 1940.)

Bert Dustin's purchase of the Teec Nos Pos Trading Post ushered in a new style of ownership. Brothers Bert and Shel Dustin, with their brothers-in-law, Al and June (Junius) Foutz, formed a partnership called the Progressive Mercantile Company which financed many of the traders on this part of the reservation, as well as supplying them with goods. Al Foutz's son, Russell, explains that Progressive would look for a young married man, give him a twenty five percent interest to run a post owned by them, and eventually buy it for himself. Sometimes one of the owners would buy a post in his own name. The Foutz family created a trading dynasty in the Four Corners area, owning more than 20 trading posts.

The four partners ran the trading post by sending two owners at a time for six month stints and did this through the 1920s. Then Luff Foutz, son of Al, ran the post. In the late 1930s, when money was short, Luff would send the best Teec Nos Pos rugs to the Rocky Mountain Park Company in Denver. Quite a few of these rugs were sold in the Denver area. Luff died from meningitis in 1939 during an epidemic on the Navajo Reservation. Ken Washburn, who had worked for Luff for many years, and Russell Foutz bought out Luff's interest and Washburn ran the post. While Washburn was managing the post in the 1930s, the Navajo rose up in protest to the government's stock reduction program. Foutz says, "I think they took the man who was the range rider at that time and they were going to lynch him, but that never

happened. At the time this was going on, Earl Saltwater (a Navajo), came into the store, told Mr. Washburn about the trouble they were having and suggested he send his wife to town. Saltwater cut the telephone lines, and Washburn's wife, no longer threatened, was released. When I first went out there to run it, that was one of the first things one of the old timers (Navajo) came in to tell me. 'I guess you know I went to the penitentiary one time for this uprising here. I wanted to tell you about it before I come in to ask for credit'."[11]

Ken Washburn left Teec Nos Pos suddenly in 1949. As a result, Russell and Helen Foutz had to move with their three small children from Fruitland to the trading post. Helen, who was city bred, reminisced about their first day, "The Indians had a nasty habit that when anybody new came as a trader, they tried to make this life just as miserable as possible. Our experience was typical. The Indians, by means of a tom-tom or other device they used, all knew that there was a new man out there. Of course they were familiar with his name, but that did not make any difference. They weren't familiar with him. They would take to coming in one at a time, buying one item. All of this was charged, of course, in those days it was all on credit. They would come in to buy a can of tomatoes and we would have to write out a slip, hand it to them and give them their tomatoes. They would go outside and stay for 15-20 minutes and they would come in to buy a can of peaches, and we would go through the whole process time after time. There were probably 3 dozen people who came in an average of 6 times during that day, each buying one item at a time. They were just testing us. But I can remember that we didn't get out of the store that night until 10 o'clock. They would come up to me and tell me what they wanted, that they wanted a sack of flour. I would have to go back into the wareroom to get a ten- or twenty-five-pound sack of flour,

According to Hamp Noel, in the 1958 interviews with Frank McNitt, The Shiprock Fair was held during late October. It had rained off and on for about a week. "We were all camped on the river bottom among the trees, just east of the old bridge. The old bridge (which was to be washed out in the flood) was just about where the new bridge is today. The exhibit was on slightly higher ground. When the river rose that night we moved and camped on Bruce Bernard's hill. In the morning I went down to where my horses were tied up and found them in water nearly up to their backs, holding their heads up out of the water. (We wanted to move) but Shelton told us we couldn't move. We had to stay right there. I had $5,000 worth of Navajo silverwork and rugs which I stood to lose. Shelton told me I couldn't move it. During the morning Harry Baldwin up at the Hogback Trading Post called up on the telephone and told my brother Frank that the river was cresting and the water was already up around his door. Frank and the rest of us packed up our exhibits, just defied Shelton who still didn't want us to move - and moved out to higher ground. If we hadn't we would have all gone broke beautifully. Yes, the Beclabito post was built from some of the timbers washed down the San Juan river in that flood. Mrs. Noel says "The water rose in Shiprock until all of the buildings were under water up to the eaves. Shingles were floating about everywhere." Photo Mc Nitt Collection, #6931. State Records Center and Archives, Santa Fe, NM.

put it on my shoulder and sling it over the counter. I tell you we were utterly exhausted at the end of that day. Things got better after that, but they had their fun with us."[12]

The Foutz family stayed at the post for several years until they moved to Farmington, NM, sixty miles away. Russell stayed on with the help of Jay and Lloyd Foutz (cousins) until Jay and Lloyd bought the nearby Beclabito Trading Post. In 1959 the Teec Nos Pos Trading Post burned. A highway was in the planning stage, so Russell tried to rebuild the post on the road. Before this time, the only access was a dirt road. "That's why it was hard to get there," Russell said, "and the Model T Fords, with their small tires, would get stuck going in. At this time the Indians had a meeting to decide whether they should let us build a trading post and continue operating there. I remember Fred Todacheenie got up at the meeting while they were discussing it and said 'all the white men cheat us, but this fellow just cheats us a little bit. I think we ought to keep him and be satisfied with the trader we have.' So there we were, trying to rebuild this trading post on a highway that wasn't even built, it was just surveyed. We would stake out the post and then they would move the highway, and this went on for several months. We did miss the corner (intersection), and so the post is not on the highway. About the time we got it finished, one salesman came out there to get an order for hardware for the store. He looked around and said, 'I'm glad my boss can't see me. If he could see me writing an order for a store that doesn't have a road going to it, I know I would be fired immediately.' "[13]

The post still operates under the aegis of the Foutz family, but the way it does business has changed. The availability of the pickup truck has given the Navajo mobility and the ability to leave the neighborhood to comparison shop their merchandise. They are no longer beholden to the local trader. They can and do shop for the best prices when selling their rugs.

The Rugs

With the change in consumer demand from blankets to rugs at the end of the 19th century, the Navajo weaving industry needed revision. The arrival of the railroad in the latter part of the 19th century brought ready-made goods at cheaper prices to the consumers of the southwest. Handwoven blankets, always important to the Navajo economy, were replaced by manufactured blankets from Pendleton Woolen Mills of Oregon. With rugs so popular in the eastern states, the traders urged the Navajo weavers to serve that market. The traders also encouraged the Navajo women to create better woven pieces which would bring them more money and actually showed them designs which would make their rugs distinctive. For example, according to Betty McGee, her father would draw rug designs, emphasize the importance of dying the wool and invite the best weavers to demonstrate weaving techniques.[14] This may have been innovative on Noel's part, although several traders, notably Will Evans at Shiprock, painted unique designs on the inside and outside walls of the trading post, hoping to influence the weavers to copy them.

Carl Steckel succinctly writes that the trader wielded enormous influence in the development of weaving. "As a business man, he developed the style and materials and encouraged the best craftsmanship. Equally, he helped shape the taste of the outside world that was paying so well for the rugs. Yet, he did this without losing sight of the fact that he was tampering with a folk art and a cultural tradition of a thousand years."[15]

The Teec Nos Pos Trading Post developed into one of the major regional clearinghouse centers. From this post we see the dissemination of two stylistic formats consisting of an outline style attributed to Red Mesa, and a style referred to by traders as geometric, with floating elements on a field. The Navajo women who frequented the post at Teec Nos Pos, according to the Foutzes, were exceptionally good weavers then and they still are today. Most of the good Teec rugs come from about five families of weavers.

The serrated, zig-zag design in which every color is outlined with a contrasting color and done in a vertical format was developed before 1905 and has not changed. Campbell, in his essay, points out that these designs are remarkably similar to the early New England flame stitch, and are identified with neighboring Red Mesa Trading Post.[16] Hedlund states that these are "clearly derived from 19th century Germantown eye-dazzler blankets."[17] Nagen thinks that the design elements of the two styles derive their basis from nature: lightning, mesa-like structures, cloud patterns and arrangements of geographic landmarks.[18]

The unique Oriental rug motifs identified with Teec Nos Pos were said to have been brought to the weavers before 1905 by a Mrs. Wilson, possibly a missionary. Noel said that the weavers themselves told him that. Russell Foutz conjectures that an itinerant artist brought sketches to the weavers, while others credit the influence of J.B. Moore at Crystal Trading Post and Ed Davies at Two Grey Hills Trading Post. This type, using Oriental carpet motifs, "has large geometric figures, often with hooked or fretted appendages arranged on a central rectangular plane and surrounded by wide, patterned borders."[19] Maxwell states that the Teec Nos Pos rug "is at once the most distinctive and least Navajo of all the reservation's specialized textile types. It is the hardest rug to place in a home... because of its complexity of design and abundance and variety of color."[20]

Foutz reports that men created designs for their wives. "Todacheenie Yazz (Little Indian) drew all the designs for his wife, who was one of the better weavers. Then Slocum Clah's son-in-law, Harry, the youngest one, would draw a lot of designs on paper and keep them in a candy showcase at the store and all the Indians would pick up or buy the designs that he would draw. The women were protective about their border designs. They would be real unhappy if some other weaver or some other family would use their borders. This border was their design and nobody else was supposed to use it."[21] Russell could look at a rug and know by the border which family had produced it, although he might not be able to identify the weaver.

Raising sheep for wool has diminished through the years. Foutz says that they used to buy about 3000 lambs each year and get 300 to 400 sacks of wool. Today, probably only half of the stores on the reservation bother with wool. When Foutz first started buying rugs for Progressive Mercantile, he said "we weighed a lot of them and the cheaper rugs we bought by the pound. But you could tell where they came from by looking at the rugs. You can't do that any more because the Indians move around so much now that they intermingle."[22]

Bill Foutz, (Russell and Helen's son, who operates a trading post in Shiprock, NM), says that, before the 1940s almost all the wool used for warp and weft was handspun and hand dyed. After World War II, the

weavers would use Redheart, a 4-ply commercial wool, and then 3-ply Germantown wool in small amounts, in filler elements. Wool skeins were stocked in limited quantity. The skeins were small. Redheart had a red heart on the wrapping. Bill continues "Unless you wanted to hand-dye all that wool yourself, it's the only wool you could get in vibrant colors, greens, the purples. Basically, Germantown is a ply wool. People don't realize that Germantown is a commercial, store-bought, store-dyed wool yarn. They think it was something special. It wasn't. It was stuff you bought right at the Ben Franklin store."[23] The availability of commercial wool was a time saver and made it easier for the weaver to concentrate on design and quality of weaving.

Bill Foutz remembers that people have always asked for classy, patterned rugs, then and now. "We made these things for other people to buy. That was the whole purpose of it. The Navajo did not own these things, and did not put them in their houses. They were and are made exclusively for export. What was made was influenced by what the trader told them to make, based on what sold well against what didn't sell well. There are a lot of reasons why heavily bordered rugs aren't made, weren't made in great numbers, even then. If you have a rug that's all border, you have no room for the center. The 1930s produced some of the best rug designs, where the weavers used a lot of filler elements. The busier it was, the more money it brought."[24] Russell Foutz sponsored a contest every year for the best weaving. Inevitably, those rugs with the fullest centers won the prizes.

Continuing some of his practical, perhaps iconoclastic, opinions, Bill talks about the weaving standards. "These rugs have to be perfect. Any flaw that you see might be charming in 30 years, but was a great detriment back then, as it is now, on any new rug.

The object was to make them as perfect as could be. You didn't want color changes, warps showing, bleeding or crooked rugs. You wanted it like a machine could do it. You got the best money. To do it otherwise caused the weaver to suffer. If there was a mistake, she knew that she made it, and she knew that she was going to take a hit on it. She might give you a long story—dah, dah, dah, this and that, or it's just a little thing, don't worry about it. Your fault, you shouldn't have sold me this color with the change in it. But that doesn't negate the fact that there is a mistake in it and it will cost."[25]

Teec Nos Pos design development approached its zenith during the 1930s and 1940s. This seems to be the golden age of weaving at Teec Nos Pos. Nagen points out that the best Teec weavings from the 1930s often exhibit a carded grey field with a bluish cast.[26] Kent states that Teec Nos Pos rugs in the 1940s are distinguished by unusual geometric motifs, not Navajo in origin, that seem to float on a solid color field. Floating motifs appear as though drawn with black lines on a gray field, often "outlined in bright colors or highlighted by the small spots of color that have earned them the name 'jewel pattern' among collectors."[27] This form has continued to the present day, but identification is no longer confined to the Teec Nos Pos area, as has been indicated earlier in the text.

Regarded as aberrant to the mainstream of Navajo designed development by scholars and collectors through the first several decades of this century, all Teec Nos Pos rugs, since the early 1980s, have surpassed even the famous Two Grey Hills in both price and demand, and are the most popular of the regional rugs.[28] According to Gilbert Maxwell, the Teec Nos Pos rugs reserve their greatest appeal for the serious collector and could be the classic weaving of the 20th century.[29]

Plate 1. Teec Nos Pos Pictorial Rug
44" x 64" circa 1915.
Early Teec rugs are characterized
by eccentric, and sometimes multiple, borders.
The inclusion of pictorial elements,
in this case corn, one of the four sacred plants,
is rare in weavings from this area.

Plate 2. Teec Nos Pos Rug
45" x 69" circa 1915-1920.
Another characteristic of early period Teec
weaving is the inclusion of large amounts of
carded camel color wool. Small sizes,
3' x 5' and 4' x 6' predominate. Bows and
arrows and feathers are associated with rain in
Navajo mythology.

Plate 3. Teec Nos Pos Rug
40" x 66 " circa 1910-1915.
Black lines connecting filler elements are
usually indicative of early period weavings,
circa 1905-1920.

Plate 4. Teec Nos Pos Rug
*50-1/2" x 84" circa 1910-1920.
In this early example, the beginning of a
later design motif, a large double cross
shape is evident.*

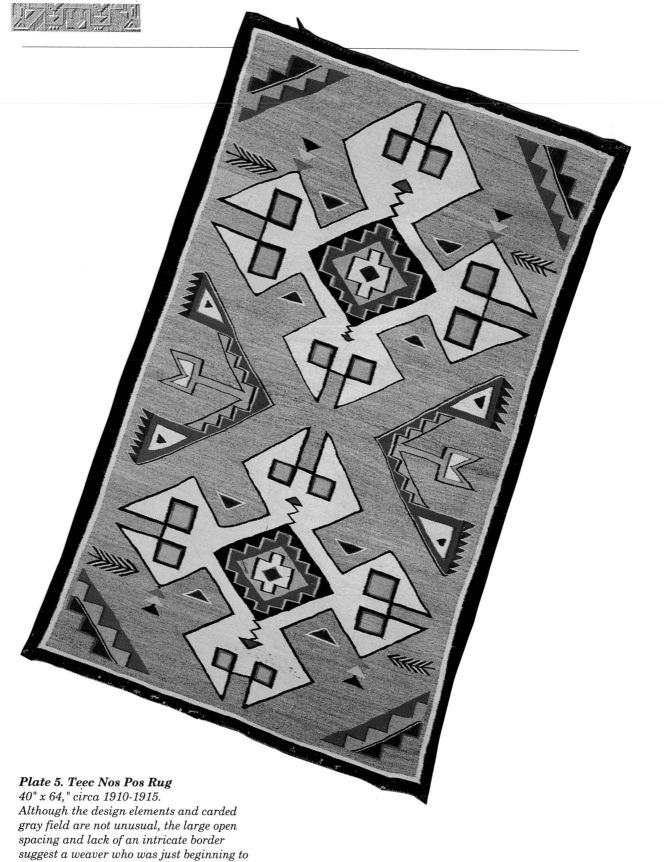

Plate 5. Teec Nos Pos Rug
40" x 64," circa 1910-1915.
Although the design elements and carded
gray field are not unusual, the large open
spacing and lack of an intricate border
suggest a weaver who was just beginning to
experiment with Teec Nos Pos design.

Plate 6. Teec Nos Pos Rug
44" x 69-1/2" circa 1915.
In this beautiful example, the weaver has
reversed the normal color arrangement.
The field is dark brown (black), while
the border is black on white.

Plate 7. Teec Nos Pos Pictorial Rug
54" x 106" circa 1915-1925.
Virtually no examples of Teec weaving have
survived which include Yei figures
(Navajo holy people). Here, three female
Yeis are set against a white ground,
surrounded by feathers. A rare example.

Plate 8. Teec Nos Pos Rug
48-1/2" x 72" circa 1935.
In this example, the center medallion has
been omitted, and the traditional mirrored
medallions have been enlarged to fill the whole field.

Plate 9. Teec Nos Pos Rug
50" x 106-1/2" circa 1920-1925.
This large, luminous floor rug perfectly exemplifies
the exhibition title, "Jewels of the Navajo Loom."
Note the inclusion of ten Vallero stars,
a design element frequently found in
rugs from this area.

Plate 10. Teec Nos Pos Rug
37-1/2" x 72" circa 1920-1925.
Although different in design, the color
palette and over-all feeling are very similar to plate 9.
Note the sophisticated use of
the double cross element.

Plate 11. Teec Nos Pos Double Saddle Blanket
32-1/2" x 54" circa 1920-1925.
The Navajo wove very few double pattern
saddle blankets and even fewer that can be
accurately attributed to the Teec Nos Pos area.
A complex and rare example.

Plate 12. Teec Nos Pos Single Saddle Blanket
27" x 35-3/4" circa 1920s.
Often referred to in the trade as 'Sunday Saddle
Blankets' these were woven as gift and trade items.
The decorative fringe and tassels are added after the
piece is removed from the loom.
Ex collection: C&G Herring.

Plate 13. Caucasian Soumak Carpet
60" x 76" circa first half 20th century.
Verbal history credits a missionary
named Mrs. Wilson with introducing Caucasian
imagery to the Teec Nos Pos weavers.
Courtesy Santa Fe Oriental Rugs.

Plate 14. Teec Nos Pos Rug
42" x 66-1/2" circa 1915-1920.
Note the remarkable similarities of design
in the border of this Navajo rug and the
Caucasian carpet in Plate 13

Plate 15. Teec Nos Pos Rug
52" x 86" circa 1940-1950.
An unusual example of a borderless Teec Nos Pos.
Note the large amount of carded brown wool.

Plate 16. Teec Nos Pos Rug
47" x 107" circa 1935-1940.
Toward the end of the 'Golden Age' of Teec Nos Pos
weaving, filler elements become fewer and more
widely spaced. In this example, the elaborate border
offsets the modest field design. The stylized
tulip-like motifs are a standard Teec design element.

Plate 17. Teec Nos Pos Runner
41-1/2" x 103" circa 1920-1930.
During the decades of the 1920s and 1930s,
Teec rugs increased in size, and filler elements
became more numerous, smaller, and increasingly
outlined in various colors.

Plate 18. Teec Nos Pos Rug
63" x 151-1/2" circa 1915-1925.
Large Teec rugs tend to be disproportionately
narrow in relationship to length. The browns
and greens are native vegetal dyes.

Plate 19. Teec Nos Pos Rug
58-1/2" x 87" circa 1925-1935.
In this Teec rug, the traditional large beige
-on-black border is dramatically offset by
an unusual meandering second inner border.

Plate 20. Teec Nos Pos Rug
55" x 81-1/2" circa 1925-1935.
A textbook example of a classic Teec border
with jewel-like elements within the tulip shapes.
As in most of this period, the filler elements
are woven with commercially plyed wool.

Plate 21. Teec Nos Pos Rug
36" x 63" circa 1915-1920.
This small rug has an extremely well-
balanced design with an exceptionally
complex border concept. Woven with a
combination of native vegetal and aniline dyes.

Plate 22. Teec Nos Pos Outline Design Rug
57" x 90" circa 1930-1940.
The serrate outline style, in which each
color is outlined with a different color, was
developed at both Red Mesa and Teec Nos Pos.
The only difference between the two is that,
at Red Mesa, the outline style has no border
or a simple, thin, solid-banded border. The Teec
weavers incorporated this style within a
tradionally elaborate Teec-bordered concept.

Plate 23. Red Mesa Outline Design Rug
57" x 92" circa 1940-1950.
A classic outline design. Historical evidence
suggests that this style may be a development
of the 19th century Germantown 'Eyedazzler'
designs, although the similarity with New England
flame stitch designs is plainly evident.
Compare with Plate 22.

***Plate 24. Red Mesa/Teec Nos Pos Third
Phase Chief Pattern Revival Rug***
*52" x 78" circa 1910-1915.
An exceptional example of an outline design
incorporated into the nine anchor points of
a traditional Third Phase Chief Pattern Rug.*

Plate 25. Teec Nos Pos Varient Rug
75" x 122" circa 1920-1935.
*Although this type of rug is generally included
in the Teec category and exhibits both Teec Nos
Pos and Crystal area elements, it could have been
woven in the Burnham area. The circular and
rosette shapes, along with the overall complexity
of design, require the skills of a master weaver.
Only a few of these have survived.
Note the two Yei figures in the center medallion.*

Fire Loss High At Trading Post

Fire Sunday completely destroyed the Tes Nos Pos Trading Post 30 miles west of Shiprock, the oldest trading post in that area. The loss was estimated in excess of $75,000.

Russell Foutz, who owns the trading post with his cousins Lloyd and Jay Foutz, said the fire broke out about 5 p.m. in the hallway between the store and the living quarters. Cause of the blaze remained unknown.

Thousands of dollars worth of pawn in turquoise, coral, silver, leather, blankets and other valuable Indian items were lost. Foutz said nothing was saved and the charred ruins were still smoldering this morning.

Foutz said the loss was partly covered by insurance, but valuable merchandise was irreplaceable.

Only the hired man, whose name was not learned, was reported at the trading post at the time this fire broke out. Lloyd and Jay operated the business, but were not there at the time, Russell said.

A missionary reportedly saw smoke and rushed to help the hired man, but their efforts to extinguish the blaze were futile.

The trading post has been in the Foutz family for years.

It was started 50 years ago by Hambleton Noel of Fruitland, father of former Farmington trustee Joy Noel. He built the trading post two years before he married Eva Foutz.

Noel was the first white man the Indians permitted to establish a trading post in that section of the reservation, and it was only through his friendship with "Blackhorse," an Indian chief, that permission was gained.

Joy Noel recalled today that his father first met "Blackhorse" while with Hyde Exploration Expedition, an archaeological party, at Pueblo Bonita. Noel had come to this country from Virginia.

Several years later, while in Farmington, Hambleton Noel loaded up a couple of wagons with merchandise and went to Tes Nos Pos to "pow wow" with the Indians about locating a trading post there.

"Blackhorse" intervened on his behalf and Noel was allowed to build a trading post.

"Dad used to tell us," Joy Noel said, "that was one time when befriending the Indians paid off."

Noel sold the trading post to Bert Dustin who sold it to Al Foutz-and several others have had it through the half century since it was started, but it's been in the Foutz family in some capacity since Hambleton Noel married Eva Foutz.

1   McNitt, *The Indian Traders,* p. 280.
2   Interview between Noel and McNitt, Fruitland, NM, January, 1958.
3   McNitt, p. 280.
4   Weeks and others, *Emigrant Cornelius Noel,* p. 289-290.
5   Interview between Noel and McNitt, Fruitland, NM, January, 1958.
6   Ibid. (The Algert store was later taken over by Progressive Mercantile Company).
7   Telephone conversation with Betty McGee, Mesa, AZ, October, 1993.
8   Interview between Noel and McNitt, Fruitland, NM, January, 1958.
9   Ibid.
10 Telephone conversation with Betty McGee, Mesa, AZ, October, 1993.
    (Although born an Episcopalian, Noel became a Mormon in
    1900, inspired by a Mormon girl. This waned, but he later
    married Eva Foutz who was a Mormon.)
11 Taped conversation with Russell Foutz, Farmington, NM, July, 1993.
12 Taped conversation with Helen Foutz, Farmington, NM, July, 1993.
13 Taped conversation with Russell Foutz, Farmington, NM, July, 1993.

Note: (1905-1913) Information in the literature is sparse. Frank McNitt has done the most compre-
    hensive research by interviewing Noel on two occasions in Fruitland, New Mexico when Noel
    was eighty-one years old. With other sources, he produced his book, *The Indian Traders.*
    References to Teec Nos Pos Trading Post in other books refer primarily to the rugs. Many
    books about the trading post era don't even mention Teec Nos Pos. The Noel family encyclo-
    pedic history, however was very helpful. I have used as many direct quotes as possible and
    credit those to McNitt's interviews with Noel, McNitt's book, and the Noel family history as
    recorded by his daughters and niece. I uncovered no new information in my research of this
    early period.

14 Conversation with Betty McGee, Mesa, AZ, 1993.
15 Steckel, p. 4-5
16 Campbell, essay.
17 Hedlund, p. 42. Hedlund also credits this style as clearly springing from the bordered
    geometric patterns when Oriental patterns were introduced to Crystal and Two
    Grey Hills communities.
18 Conversation with Nagen, Corrales, NM, December, 1993.
19 Kent, p. 89.
20 Maxwell, p. 23.
21 Taped interview with Russell Foutz, Farmington, NM, July, 1993.
22 Ibid.
23 Taped interview with Bill Foutz, Farmington, NM, July, 1993.
    Germantown is a genre name for the synthetic dyed yarns sent to the Navajo from mills
    in Germantown, PA, the last quarter of the 19th century.
24 Ibid.
25 Ibid.
26 Conversation with Nagen, Corrales, NM, December, 1993.
27 Kent, p. 89.
28 Campbell, essay.
29 Maxwell, p.23.

Bibliography

Anderson, Lowell Edgar. *Factors Influencing Design in Navajo Weaving.* Master's Thesis (Decorative Arts), Berkeley, University of California, 1951.

Campbell, Tyrone D. *The Teec Nos Pos Regional Rug, 1905-1945.* Scottsdale, Gallery 10, February 1990. (Exhibition essay).

Coolidge, Dane and Mary Roberts. *The Navajo Indians,* New York, Houghton Mifflin Co., 1930.

Hedlund, Ann L. *Reflections Of The Weavers' World,* Denver, Denver Art Museum, 1992.

Hill, Willard W. *Navajo Trading and Trading Ritual: A Study of Cultural Dynamics,* Southwestern Journal of Anthropology, Vol. IV, no. 4, 1948: 371-396.

James, H.L. *Rugs and Posts, The Story of Navajo Rugs and Their Homes,* Globe, AZ, Southwest Parks and Monuments Association, 1976.

Kaufman, Alice and Christopher Selser. *Navajo Weaving Traditions: 1650-Present.* New York, E.P. Dutton, 1985.

Kent, Kate Peck. *Navajo Weaving, Three Centuries of Change.* Santa Fe, School of American Research, 1985.

McNitt, Frank. *The Indian Traders.* Norman, University of Oklahoma Press, 1962.

Maxwell, Gilbert. *Navajo Rugs, Past, Present and Future.* Palm Desert, CA, Best West Publications, 1963.

Steckel, Carl. *Early Day Trader with the Navajo (a Brief History of an Early Day Trader with the Navajos).* El Paso, TX, [publisher unknown], 1987.

Utley, Robert M. *The Reservation Trader in Navajo History.* Santa Fe, *El Palacio,* Vol 68 (1) 1961; 5-27.

Weeks, Jennie N., Betty N. McGee and Martha N.Wilson. *Emigrant Cornelius Noel; From Holland to Virginia and his Descendants in America.* Vol. V, part IV, Book II. Salt Lake City, UT: [publisher unknown], 1980.

Note: Oral history was a principal source of information from 1913 to the present. The Foutz family provided this history of the Teec Nos Pos Trading Post.

This Book was set in New Century School Book,
Normal, Bold, and Italic.

Graphic Design and Pre-Press
production for this book were performed by
The New Valliant Company,
Albuquerque, New Mexico.

The original blanket
photography was provided by
Robert Sherwood.

Printing of this book took place at
The New Valliant Company,
Albuquerque, New Mexico.

The rug pattern used throughout
the book in the upper corners is
from the rug border of plate number 4.

This book was published by
Adobe Gallery
Albuquerque, New Mexico